# FREELY
# FORGIVEN
## A STUDY ON REDEMPTION

## BIBLE STUDIES TO IMPACT THE LIVES
## OF ORDINARY PEOPLE

Christian Focus Publications

The Word Worldwide

Written by Marie Dinnen

# PREFACE
## GEARED FOR GROWTH

'Where there's LIFE there's GROWTH:
Where there's GROWTH there's LIFE.'

*WHY GROW a study group?*

*Because as we study the Bible and share together we can*

- learn to combat loneliness, depression, staleness, frustration, and other problems
- get to understand and love each other
- become responsive to the Holy Spirit's dealing and obedient to God's Word

*and that's GROWTH.*

*How do you GROW a study group?*

- Just start by asking a friend to join you and then aim at expanding your group.
- Study the set portions daily (they are brief and easy: no catches).
- Meet once a week to discuss what you find.
- Befriend others, both Christians and non Christians, and work away together

*see how it GROWS!*

*WHEN you GROW ...*

This will happen at school, at home, at work, at play, in your youth group, your student fellowship, women's meetings, mid-week meetings, churches and communities,

*you'll be REACHING THROUGH TEACHING*

# INTRODUCTORY STUDY

The subject of 'Redemption' is a mystery to many. Why did the human race need to be redeemed? From what? Here are some typical reactions of different people when approached on the subject.

Mr A. Vrijman: 'Hey, what ya talking about? I'm as good as the rest. Give folk a helping hand. Don't commit any outrageous sins. Reckon God'll overlook a few human errors. No one's perfect.'

Mrs D. Vout: 'Me? I'm very religious. I read the Bible most nights, and go to church Sundays. I'm president of the Ladies' Guild, and I sing in the choir. I think God will quite approve of the way I live.'

Sir Lee: 'Mind your own business and I'll mind mine.'

Ms Agnes Tick: 'Well, after all, no one's come back to prove to us there's a God or afterlife. The Russian astronauts say they didn't see Him up there in outer space! Enjoying this life's good enough for me.'

Miss B. Tolrant: 'So many religions in the world. There's good in all of them – Eastern religions, new cults, the lot. All lead to the same goal. Can't be narrow-minded.'

Judge Mentle: 'Christianity? The church is full of hypocrites. Plenty of just as decent people outside of it. No thanks. I've no time for phonies.'

This series of studies is to help ordinary folk, like the six friends above, to understand the greatest subject on earth. And if you are a Christian it may help you to see in greater depth the wonder of the subject which the writer of Hebrews referred to as 'so great salvation'. We shall seek to look at it from every possible angle, and so to understand and enter more fully into the complete provision God has made for us.

Away back in the dawn of history, God made man in His own image, perfect in body, mind and spirit. He wanted to enjoy fellowship with him. He created him to rule the earth. But sin entered and all was ruined. Satan usurped the authority that man was meant to exercise on the earth. In seeking to be free from God's rule, he came into slavery to Satan, and with that slavery came sin, fear, depressions, sicknesses and a host of miseries.

God could not leave things in that state. Already He had devised a plan, a wonderful plan, by which man could be redeemed from Satan's domination, and be restored to the condition in which God originally created him. That is what redemption is all about. Various facets of the extent of redemption will be explored in the next ten studies.

Discuss the reactions of the six people mentioned above and others you may have come up against, and say what is wrong with this kind of reasoning.

One exquisite picture of someone being 'redeemed' in a physical sense is given in the story of HOSEA, in the Old Testament. It will help us understand the meaning of the word 'redemption' and prepare us for our study.

Look up:

Hosea 1:2-3   What did the Lord tell Hosea his wife would be like?
Hosea 2:2     What do we discover about Hosea's wife here?
Hosea 3:1-3   What can we deduce about Gomer from these verses (especially v. 2)?

In the musical, *Hosea*, written by a Salvation Army captain, you listen to the money-loving auctioneer selling off his slaves in the market. Gomer is the one being displayed at the time, and the sordid nature of the whole set-up is very evident.

When Hosea comes to buy back his erring wife, makes the highest bid and pays the price, the noisy crowd is reduced to silence as they realise the emotional depths of what has just taken place.

In hushed tones they say:

What amazing love! Can it really be?
Can our eyes believe what they seem to see?
Can a man forgive? Can a man forget?
No, I can't believe it's true –
And yet ... and yet ... and yet ...

What amazing love indeed, for Hosea to go down into the degradation of the slave market, to buy back a woman who had treated him abominably, but whom, incredibly, he still loved.

Discuss the spiritual parallel.

# STUDY 1

## THE NEED FOR IT

## QUESTIONS

**DAY 1** *Genesis 1:26-28; 2:7, 15, 18-25.*
a) By what means did God create –
1. Adam?
2. Eve?
b) In what condition spiritually, mentally and physically did He create man? Give evidence of this.

**DAY 2** *Genesis 2:16-17.*
a) What one test did Adam and Eve face?
b) What was to be the punishment for disobedience?

**DAY 3** *Genesis 3:1-5.*
What did the serpent say to cause Eve to doubt:
a) the truth of God's word?
b) God's love and care for them?

**DAY 4** *Genesis 3:6; 1 John 2:16.*
a) In what three areas of Eve's being did the tempter attack her? (Compare the areas in which Satan later tempted Jesus, Matt. 4:1-11)
b) Giving in to any of these forms of temptation can be summed up in one word. What is it?

**DAY 5** *Genesis 3:6-12, 16-19, 23-24; 4:1-8.*
How did their giving in to temptation affect:
a) their relationship with God?
b) their relationship with each other?
c) their first-born son?
d) What punishment did God mete out to each of them?

**DAY 6** *Genesis 2:16-17; Romans 5:12, 17a, 18a, 19a, 21a; 6:23a.*
a) How do the 'Romans' references describe the consequences of this act of disobedience?
b) God had decreed that on the day they ate the fruit they would surely die. How was this fulfilled in them?

# QUESTIONS (contd.)

**DAY 7** *Genesis 3:15, 21.*

God's holiness obliged Him to punish sin, but His love caused Him to plan for man's redemption. How is this implied vaguely here? (We will enlarge on this subject next week.)

# NOTES

Before we can fully understand the need for God to redeem the world, we must consider two things:

## I. THE CHARACTER OF GOD

Our human minds cannot begin to grasp the wonder of the attributes of our Creator God. Indeed, we could not endure a revelation of His glory. Even the sight of an angel of God brought terror to many saints of Bible days. How much more if we, in our present state, should really see God. Let's look at a few things the Bible reveals about Him.

> a. He is OMNIPOTENT. That means He can do everything. Since He created the universe, nothing is too difficult for Him to do.
> b. He is OMNISCIENT. He has complete knowledge and wisdom. Science is just beginning to unravel the fringe of His great wisdom.
> c. He is OMNIPRESENT. He is present at the farthest away galaxy of X million light years from little planet earth, and yet He is present in every situation right here. He sees every sparrow that falls to the ground.
> d. He is HOLY. Pure whiteness that we could never look upon.
> e. Yet He is perfect LOVE, compassion and mercy. Man, made in God's image is unique, the peak of all God's creative genius. And what a glorious world God created for man to enjoy! His love flowed out towards man. That love is still flowing out – towards every man, woman and child – towards you!

## 2. THE CHARACTER OF MAN

In today's study we see that this glorious, wise, holy God created man in perfection, to be a companion for Himself, to be obedient and loving to Him. But disobedience and rebellion brought about a separation from God. God could not be holy and continue in fellowship with those who had chosen to defy Him. Yet, because of His love, He set about finding a means of forgiveness, reconciliation and restoration. If Adam and Eve became sinners, how much more their progeny of today: rebellion, blasphemy, and mocking of God have reached epidemic proportions. YET God still loves man, and His love and mercy extend even to those who hate Him.

In today's study we see man's need of redemption. In further studies we shall see unfolded God's means of bringing this about.

*MEMORY VERSE:*
There is no difference, for all have sinned and fall short of the glory of God
(Rom. 3:22b, 23).

# STUDY 2
## PICTURES FROM THE OLD TESTAMENT

## QUESTIONS

**DAY 1** *Genesis 22:1-2; John 3:16.*
a) Who was Abraham prepared to offer as a sacrifice?
b) How does this parallel what God did for us?

**DAY 2** *Genesis 22:3-8; John 19:17; 2 Corinthians 5:19; Philippians 2:8.*
a) Isaac carried the wood on which he was to be sacrificed. How is even this a picture of Jesus?
b) Twice we are told that 'the two of them (father and son) went on together'. In what way can this apply to the sacrifice of Jesus?
c) Do you think Isaac was 'obedient unto death' just like Jesus was (Phil. 2:8)?

**DAY 3** *Genesis 22:9-13; Luke 23:46; Hebrews 11:17-19.*
a) How does this part of the story differ from Jesus' sacrifice?
b) How is this story a picture of the resurrection of Jesus?

**DAY 4** *Exodus 12:1-6; 1 Peter 1:19.*
a) Describe the lamb the people were to sacrifice. How is it a picture of the Lord Jesus?
b) How does this story show us that it is not just the good life of Jesus but also His death that saves us?

**DAY 5** *Exodus 12:7-13; Hebrews 10:22; John 6:56-57; Colossians 1:27.*
a) What significance was there in the act of applying the blood?
b) They had to eat the flesh of the lamb. How does this apply to our relationship with Jesus?

**DAY 6** *Exodus 12:14-20; 1 Corinthians 11:23-26.*
a) What celebration that most Christians keep compares with this Jewish Feast of Passover?
b) 1 Corinthians 5:6-8. Remembering that yeast (leaven) in the Bible is a type of sin, what can we learn from these verses?

**DAY 7** *Exodus 12:29-51; Deuteronomy 7:8; Ephesians 1:3.*
a) They went out with great wealth. What spiritual meaning can this have for us?
b) From what did God redeem the Israelite nation? How can we apply this to ourselves?

# NOTES

Throughout the Old Testament, redemption through the coming Redeemer, the Lord Jesus, is constantly implied. In fact, the central theme of the Old Testament is 'sacrifice', leading up to, and preparing the people for, the sacrifice of Jesus Christ on the cross.

All sacrifices laid down in the Law of Moses – the Burnt Offering, the Cereal Offering, the Peace Offering, the Sin Offering and the Guilt Offering (Lev. 1–5) – are pictures of the coming sacrifice of Jesus, the Lamb of God.

Jesus' sacrifice is also pictured in historical incidents that took place hundreds of years before His coming. We look today at two of these.

## 1. THE OFFERING OF ISAAC – Genesis 22
God had promised Abraham a son through whom the whole human race would be blessed. His wife Sarah later gave birth to a son, Isaac, when she was 90 and he 100 years old. What a precious son! Then, when Isaac was a young man, God asked Abraham to offer this son as a sacrifice. Can you try to imagine the heartbreak, yet the perfect trust and obedience, as Abraham ascended the hill where his son was to be sacrificed? And can you visualise the 'Gethsemane' Isaac went through as his old father told him of God's command? He chose to submit, to be willing to offer himself as a burnt offering to God. What a picture of Jesus! For Isaac a substitute was found, but not for Jesus, Son of Isaac and Son of God.

## 2. THE PASSOVER – Exodus 12
The nation of Israel had been enslaved by the Egyptians for over 400 years. Then God raised up a deliverer in Moses. After inflicting many plagues on Egypt in order to force the nation to release Israel, God resorted to a final judgment. At midnight the first-born of all the land of Egypt would die. But for Israel there was redemption. Each family was to slay a lamb, and apply the blood to the lintel and doorposts of the house. They were to remain indoors, and eat the roasted flesh of the lamb in preparation for flight. At midnight the Angel of Death struck. But those protected by the sign of the blood were safe. The Egyptians capitulated. And early morning saw the nation of Israel, strengthened by the flesh of the lamb, and protected by the blood, marching out of Egypt into freedom. Can you see in this passover lamb a picture of Jesus Christ, the Lamb of God?

*MEMORY VERSE:*
For you know that it was not with perishable things such as silver or gold that you were redeemed ... but with the precious blood of Christ, a lamb without blemish or defect (1 Pet. 1:18-19).

REDEMPTION • STUDY 2 • PICTURES FROM THE OLD TESTAMENT • • • • • •

# STUDY 3

## THE SACRIFICE OF JESUS

## QUESTIONS

**DAY 1** *Matthew 16:21; 20:18-19; 26:2; Mark 10:45.*
a) What did Jesus tell His disciples about His coming sufferings?
b) From these predictions of Jesus, how do we see that Jesus did not merely die a martyr's death, as so many others have done?

**DAY 2** *Luke 23:1-4,13-15, 22.*
a) What was Pilate's verdict concerning Jesus' guilt or innocence?
b) What was Jesus' own claim (John 8:29, 46)?

**DAY 3** *Isaiah 52:14; 53:3, 4.*
Much of the teaching concerning the reason for Christ's sufferings comes from the Old Testament.
a) What do Isaiah 52:14 and 53:3 tell us of His physical and mental sufferings?
b) What does Isaiah 53:4 tell us of His spiritual sufferings?

**DAY 4** *Isaiah 53:4-8.*
a) What reasons does Isaiah give for His sufferings?
b) How did Jesus react to His sufferings (Matt. 27:14; John 19:8-10)?

**DAY 5** *Isaiah 53:9; Matthew 27:38, 57-60; John 19:33-37.*
a) How was this prophecy in Isaiah fulfilled for Jesus?
b) How can we be sure that Jesus really did die on the cross, and did not just faint, as some believe?

**DAY 6** *Isaiah 53:10-12.*
a) What hint is there here of Jesus' resurrection?
b) What did Jesus gain as a result of His sacrifice? And what do we gain?

# QUESTIONS (contd.)

**DAY 7** *I Corinthians 15:3-8, 14-21.*

a) Paul gives an incomplete list of folk to whom Christ appeared after His resurrection. List these and any others you can cull from the Gospels.

b) Why is the fact of Christ's bodily resurrection so vital to the subject of His sacrifice on the cross?

# NOTES

We come now to the Holy of Holies in our study course. We have seen how God created man in His own image, to have fellowship with Himself, and to have authority on earth. We have seen how Satan, who himself had fallen through rebellion and pride, led our first parents into the same error. Fellowship with God was broken. Man became corrupt, with a bias towards sin and self-centredness. Satan usurped the authority Adam was meant to have and Adam became his slave. And the judgment for disobedience, physical and spiritual death, came upon him. And WE are Adam's children, born with his nature.

But even before the need arose, God in His foreknowledge had already planned to provide a Redeemer. The Redeemer had to be sinless. He had to be all love and compassion. And He must be a man. No angel could qualify. Only God is completely holy, completely loving and compassionate. Therefore, God Himself must become man in order to redeem the sons of men.

Jesus, the Son of God, became man. He came in a truly human body, subject to every human test and temptation. But He lived His life in complete dependence on the Father, delighting to do the will of God, and remained unspotted by sin.

Yet, as a human being there were battles to face, the greatest being that which He faced in the Garden of Gethsemane the evening before His crucifixion. The horror of the physical and mental sufferings came before Him – the betrayal, rejection, lashing, mockery and death by being nailed to a cross. But that was not all. Jesus knew that the punishment for sin was also spiritual death, separation from fellowship with the Father, a separation which wrung the agonised cry from Him on the cross, 'My God, my God, why have you forsaken me?' In the Garden of Gethsemane, Jesus faced the cost of your salvation and mine, and, as always, His answer was, 'Father ... not as I will, but as you will'.

The next day Jesus went through it all, not only bearing our punishment but also our sin, that we might go free. And from the cross came the triumphant cry, 'It is finished!' The way of salvation was now open to all the sons of men.

Praise God, after the cross with all its horror, came the resurrection. Jesus came back to assure us that the work of redemption was completed. The way to fellowship with the Father was now open to the whole human race.

*MEMORY VERSE:*
We all, like sheep, have gone astray, each of us has turned to his own way;
and the LORD has laid on him the iniquity of us all (Isa. 53:6).

REDEMPTION • STUDY 3 • THE SACRIFICE OF JESUS

12

# STUDY 4

## OUR SIDE OF IT

### QUESTIONS

**DAY 1** *Command to repent: Matthew 3:1-2, 8; 4:17; Acts 2:38; 20:21; 26:20.*
a) What message, emphasised by both Jesus and John the Baptist, is still the message every true evangelist must preach today?
b) What does Matthew 3:8 mean?

**DAY 2** *Repentance as a condition of forgiveness: Proverbs 28:13; Matthew 6:14-15; Luke 24:47; 2 Corinthians 7:10; 1 John 1:8-9.*
a) Find out the meaning of the word 'repentance' in a dictionary. The Greek word 'metanoia' translated 'repentance' means a change of heart towards God and towards sin. Does this go beyond the dictionary meaning?
b) Can anyone receive forgiveness without turning away from sin?
c) Which particular sin is specially mentioned as keeping us back from receiving forgiveness?

**DAY 3** *Luke 15:11-24.*
a) What steps did the prodigal son take that proved his repentance?
b) What was the result of his repentance?

**DAY 4** *John 3:16; 5:24; Acts 16:30-34; 20:21; Romans 10:9-10.*
a) What next step is closely associated with repentance?
b) How does this 'saving faith' go beyond 'head belief'?

**DAY 5** *John 1:11-12; Revelation 3:20.*
a) What is another word for 'believing in' Jesus?
b) If you 'receive' Jesus, or 'open the door' to Him, what will He do?

**DAY 6** *Matthew 10:32; Acts 2:38; Romans 10:9-10; 1 John 4:15.*
a) Having truly repented, believed on or received Jesus into your life, what further steps will make your salvation real to you?
b) What should you say to others concerning Jesus?

## QUESTIONS (contd.)

**DAY 7** *Luke 10:20; John 3:16; 1 Peter 1:8-9; 1 John 5:13.*
a) Having repented and put your faith in Jesus, why is it not presumptuous to affirm that you know you have eternal life?
b) Does God confirm our faith with feelings of joy and praise? Is it our feelings that are the guide to knowing that we have been saved, or is it the promises in the Word of God?
c) Do you KNOW that you have received this great gift of salvation?

# NOTES

Let's illustrate with two stories:

1. KAREN is a teenager with a background of a loving, stable home. As a child she was always happy and enjoyed a good relationship with her parents. Now, as a teenager, she gets into bad company and finds herself living a double life. At home, deception and lies. She is going to her girlfriend's to study with her, but the evening finds her engaging in a very different way of life. Her pocket money is no longer sufficient, and mother wonders why her housekeeping money doesn't go as far as it should. Suspicion, tension, more lies, more rebellion. Two worried parents, one guilt-ridden daughter and involvement with the police.

Now Karen knows that the only way to peace in her heart and in her home is to leave the friends who have led her astray, make a clean breast of everything to her parents, and ask for their forgiveness. As the tearful confession is made, Karen finds herself in the arms of an equally tearful mother. There is forgiveness, reconciliation and the joy of knowing that she is not rejected, but received and loved. A new life begins for Karen.

2. Two lads are gazing at Tom's new bike. 'Isn't it just wonderful Tom! How I'd love one, but my Dad could never afford it.' Dad, sitting by the open window, hears the conversation and glances out to see such a look of longing in his Johnnie's eyes. 'I wonder, could we possibly manage one for his birthday?' Months of loving self-sacrifice. The big day comes and Johnnie is escorted down to the garage, to find himself gazing at a beautiful new bike. Then the truth dawns. It is his – his very own! Young arms are flung around Dad's neck. Excited thanks. And Johnnie is off to try out his own new bike. Oh, what joy!

These two simple stories show us how we can receive the greatest of all gifts, the gift of salvation.

First, there must be REPENTANCE. Faith without true repentance is only a mental assent and is sterile. Like Karen, we must be truly sorry and confess our sins to God, and with all our heart turn away from the thing that cost Jesus His very life's blood.

Then we must RECEIVE God's gift and thank Him for it. Johnnie realised the love and sacrifice involved in his parents' gift, and with joy and thanksgiving received it. So with God's far greater gift of salvation. It involved great sacrifice and inexpressible love. We cannot work for it. We can only receive it with joy and thanksgiving.

And the result? Forgiveness, reconciliation, peace, a clean heart and the joy of knowing that we have truly received the greatest of all gifts, the Lord Jesus Christ Himself.

REDEMPTION • STUDY 4 • OUR SIDE OF IT

· · · · · · ·
·  ·

# STUDY 5
## THE WORK OF GOD IN REDEMPTION

## QUESTIONS

**DAY 1** *John 16:7-9; Acts 11:18; Ephesians 2:8.*
a) What work would God the Holy Spirit do in the world?
b) How do Acts 11:18 and Ephesians 2:8 show that repentance and faith are also brought about by God?

**DAY 2** *John 1:13; 3:5-8; 1 Peter 1:23.*
a) According to these verses, what happens to us when we receive Jesus?
b) Who is the one who brings this miracle about?
c) Luke 1:35. The birth of Jesus was brought about by the overshadowing of the Holy Spirit upon Mary. How is this a beautiful picture of our spiritual birth?

**DAY 3** *Luke 10:20; Revelation 3:5; 20:15; 21:27; Romans 8:15-17.*
a) What record does God make when we receive salvation?
b) What inner witness do we receive in our spirits?

**DAY 4** *John 14:15-17; Romans 8:9; 1 Corinthians 6:19-20; Ephesians 3:16-19.*
a) When we receive salvation, who comes to live within us?
b) What difference should this knowledge make to us?

**DAY 5** *John 14:26; 15:26; 16:13-14; 1 John 2:27.*
What did Jesus say that the Holy Spirit, the Comforter, would do when He comes to live in us?

**DAY 6** *Galatians 5:22-23; Hebrews 13:15.*
The Holy Spirit begins to change our characters. What are some of the traits of Jesus that He brings about in us?

**DAY 7** *John 14:6; Acts 4:12; Isaiah 43:11.*
a) We often hear people say that all religions lead to God. How do we know that this is not true?
b) What makes Christianity entirely different from every other religion in its teaching on salvation?

# NOTES

THE TRINITY – this is an unusual word, and difficult to explain. God is one and yet He reveals Himself to us in three manifestations, and all are at work in redeeming us from sin and bringing us into a relationship with God.

God the Father planned our redemption and sent the Son, the Lord Jesus Christ, into the world to redeem us.

Jesus the Son became man and sacrificed Himself for us.

The Holy Spirit was sent into the world to make all the aspects of this wonderful salvation real to us and to bring us into the experience of salvation.

Sometimes the Bible speaks of God (Phil. 2:13) or Christ (Col. 1:27) or the Holy Spirit (I Cor. 6:19, 20) living and working in us. The important thing for us to understand is that all heaven is bent on bringing the whole human race into the Kingdom of God. Even the angels rejoice over one sinner who repents.

Many of the references this week have considered the work of the Holy Spirit in bringing about our salvation. We have seen our need to repent and trust Jesus, yet we cannot do even this without the Holy Spirit enabling us. It is He who makes us feel bad about the wrong in our lives, and leads us to trust in Jesus. Even so, He will never override our free wills – He won't force us to repent and believe. We have to choose to do this. And when we make that choice, it is He who causes us to be born into the family of God, and brings us into relationship with the Father. Through His work in us we become a part of the new creation – the Kingdom of God on earth.

So, we see that redemption is not one-sided. It is a co-operation between God and ourselves. All that God looks for in us is a desire to know Him. Then the Holy Spirit takes steps to bring us into that glorious experience of salvation. He enables us to repent and turn to Jesus; He brings us into the family of God, and then sets about bringing that family likeness into our lives. Let us yield our lives completely to Him that He may be free to bring this glorious work about within us.

Come, thou everlasting Spirit, bring to every thankful mind
All the Saviour's dying merit, all His sufferings for mankind.
True recorder of His passion, now the living faith impart,
Now reveal His great salvation into every faithful heart.

*MEMORY VERSE:*
But when he, the Spirit of truth, comes, he will guide you into all truth ... He will bring glory to me by taking from what is mine and making it known to you
(John 16:13-14).

# STUDY 6
## THE GREAT EXCHANGE

## QUESTIONS

**DAY 1** *2 Corinthians 5:17-18.*
a) Suggest some of the 'old' things which pass away when we come into relationship with Christ.
b) What has happened to the separation that sin had brought about between God and man?

**DAY 2** *Romans 5:1, 9, 16, 19; Isaiah 53:4, 5; 1 Peter 2:24.*
a) The word 'justification' means being declared righteous in God's sight. How does this go beyond forgiveness?
b) How is this justification brought about?
c) The references above from Isaiah and 1 Peter indicate that Jesus' sacrifice makes provision for our body too. Comment on this.

**DAY 3** *Romans 5:17.*
a) What wonderful exchanges do we see in this verse?
b) What is our part in this transaction?

**DAY 4** *Galatians 2:15-16; 5:1.*
a) Can we earn forgiveness by attempting to keep the Old Testament law?
b) After receiving Christ's salvation, why is it that we can be sure that we will never be condemned for our sins? (John 5:24; Rom. 5:9; 8:1)

**DAY 5** *Galatians 3:13-14; 2 Corinthians 8:9.*
What two exchanges, through the grace of our Lord Jesus Christ, do we see here?

**DAY 6** *John 3:16; 10:10; Romans 5:17; Colossians 3:4.*
What kind of life does Christ give us in place of the death we deserved?

# QUESTIONS (contd.)

**DAY 7** a) Make a list in two columns: one with the negative things Christ takes from us, the other with the positive blessings He gives us in their place.

b) Evaluate how far YOU have entered into this exchange. Are there aspects of it you need to trust God to work into your experience?

# NOTES

Today we looked more fully into the dire consequences of Adam's sin, and saw in Christ's redemption how all these tragic consequences have been overcome for the believer.

## CONSEQUENCES TO THE HUMAN RACE OF ADAM'S FALL

### 1. A Change in the Nature of Man
God had created man in His own image. Sin entered and now Adam and Eve, instead of loving God, feared Him and hid from Him. They became sinners and the whole human race has inherited this tendency to sin. Their first-born son became a murderer; we have become a race of rebels.

### 2. Death: Spiritual and Physical
Adam and Eve died spiritually, that is, their relationship with God was severed at the moment of their sin. Physical decay, too, started from that moment and ended in death 930 years later. Sin causes spiritual and physical death in their offspring also.

### 3. Loss of Authority
Adam had been created to have authority in the earth (Gen. 1:26). Then Satan deceived him and usurped that authority. Therefore, through the ages, Satan has been able to bring man into temptations, doubts, fears, illnesses and depressions.

### 4. God's Curse
Man came under the curse, resulting in God's judgment on him, which leads to eternal separation from God.

## EXCHANGES CHRIST HAS BROUGHT ABOUT THROUGH HIS REDEMPTION

### 1. A New Nature
The life of Christ within us in place of the old rebellious nature given to us by Adam. In place of our sins, we now receive Christ's righteousness (Rom. 5:17).

### 2. Life
Abundant, eternal life, instead of death (John 10:10, 28; 11:25-26).

### 3. Authority
Authority over Satan, instead of him having authority over us (Luke 10:19).

### 4. God's Blessing
His blessing on our lives instead of His curse. The fear of death and of judgment are removed (Gal. 3:9; Heb. 2:15).

God wants to restore His people to the place Adam and Eve occupied before sin entered the world. Impossible? Not from God's side. But first we must be convinced that God has made full provision and then co-operate with Him by faith and surrender to His will, so as to enter progressively more fully into it.

*MEMORY VERSE:*
Therefore, if anyone is in Christ, he is a new creation; the old has gone, the new has come! (2 Cor. 5:17).

# STUDY 7

## CHANGE OF OWNERSHIP

## QUESTIONS

**DAY 1** *Luke 4:18; Acts 26:18; 1 Corinthians 6:19-20; Colossians 1:13.*
a) What did Jesus claim He had come to do?
b) From what state, and into what state, does Christ transfer His people?
c) From God's point of view, when did this transfer take place?

**DAY 2** *Romans 6:6, 11-14, 16.*
a) What is one aspect of Satan's slavery from which Christ delivers us?
b) What can we do to continually enjoy this new liberty?

**DAY 3** *Romans 6:22-23.*
a) What wages does Satan give his slaves?
b) And what reward does Christ give to those who have found freedom in Him?

**DAY 4** *Galatians 2:16; 3:1-11; 4:8-9; 5:1.*
a) Why were the Galatians described as being 'foolish'?
b) What, in these verses, is the opposite of trying to keep the law?
c) What counsel does Paul give to those who are tempted to go back into slavery to the law?

**DAY 5** *Romans 8:1-4, 13-15.*
a) Instead of being led by the letter of the law, by whom are we now free to be led?
b) Suggest some man-made laws that might keep Christians of today bound to traditions and hinder the leading of God's Spirit.

**DAY 6** *Romans 8:15-16; 2 Timothy 1:7; Hebrews 2:14-15;*
a) Satan keeps his slaves in a state of fear. What replaces this fear for those whom Christ has redeemed?
b) Into what new relationship with God does freedom from slavery to Satan bring us?

**DAY 7** *John 13:13; 14:15,23; Philippians 2:9-11.*
If we recognise that we have been redeemed from slavery to the tyrant Satan, what must our attitude be to our Redeemer?

TOM: 'Hey, Joe, heard the exciting news? The government has passed a law saying that slavery is finished. Brother, we're free! We can just walk right out of this plantation, and ol' master can't stop us. Oh, boy!'

JOE: 'Don't believe it, mate. Our master wouldn't let us go. Not he.'

TOM: 'We're legally free. He can't stop us. We can go and get a job at the mill for good pay, and start a whole new life. Come, mate.'

JOE: 'Not for me. I don't know that I believe it. I know he'd come after me and bring me back. Anyway, I've sort of got used to this way of life. No, I'm secure here. I'll stay put. You go. Not for me.'

Can you imagine this kind of conversation taking place when the Law of Emancipation has been passed in any country? Of one thing you can be sure: the slave master would try to prevent his slaves from hearing about the new law, and would use all his wiles to retain them in his power. And, like Joe, there would be slaves who would not be prepared to try out the adventure of living as free men.

In this spiritual life, man was in slavery to Satan from the days of the Garden of Eden. Now, through Christ's redemption, the Law of Emancipation has been passed. Many Christians are unaware of the fact that they are free from the old slavery. Others, after hearing, find it too big to grasp. It's too difficult to muster the faith to walk out into freedom, and they feel a bit secure in retaining some of the old ways; they remain slaves to besetting sins, fears, and self-pity. What they don't grasp is that, in becoming free from the old master, they are not walking out into a void, but into a life of loving service directed by the new Master, the Lord Jesus Christ.

Let's look at a couple of verses in Luke 11:21, 22. Jesus describes Satan as 'a strong man, fully armed guarding his goods'. He seems unassailable, but then what happens? One who is stronger than he is overcomes him. When Jesus gave His life to redeem us, He overcame the tyrant. And then:

1. He takes away the armour in which the strong man trusted.
2. He divides the spoil.

So, though Satan is still alive and well on Planet Earth, for the Christian he is now unarmed! And what is more, Jesus recovered all that Satan took from man at the Fall and has given it to us. We have the armour. Read about it in Ephesians 6:10-16. So Satan only works by bluff and we can resist him.

Of course, all this presupposes that we recognise Jesus' authority over our lives in place of Satan's. If we don't, we open ourselves to Satan's attacks. When we submit ourselves utterly to Jesus' authority, then not only can we stand against Satan's attacks on ourselves, but we can use the authority of our captain, Jesus, to rescue others from Satan's kingdom.

The old master's one aim is to bring people down to hell. The new Master's aim is to rescue us from every vestige of Satan's power, but we must co-operate in this.

*MEMORY VERSE:*

It is for freedom that Christ has set us free. Stand firm, then, and do not let yourselves be burdened again by a yoke of slavery (Gal. 5:1).

# STUDY 8

## UNION WITH CHRIST

## QUESTIONS

**DAY 1** *1 Corinthians 6:15-17; 2 Corinthians 11:2; Ephesians 5:25-27; Hosea 2:19-20.*
True marriage is a covenant between two people. Comment on how this applies to our relationship with Christ.

**DAY 2** *Matthew 11:29.*
a) How is union with Christ depicted in this verse?
b) Do we automatically know how to work under the yoke with Christ, or does it require training?
c) Does it lead to frustration or restfulness?

**DAY 3** *John 15:1-11.*
Meditate on this passage, and answer these questions, stating the verse that gives the answer.
a) On what does bearing fruit depend?
b) What is another by-product of abiding (or remaining) in Christ?
c) How can a Christian experience fullness of joy?

**DAY 4** *1 John 1:3; 2:24, 27; Ephesians 3:16, 19.*
a) With whom may you continually enjoy fellowship, according to these verses?
b) How is this a two-way fellowship?

**DAY 5** *Romans 6:3-11; Ephesians 2:4-6; 4:22-24.*
a) The picture here is of identification with Christ. I (i.e. my old sinful self) was crucified and buried with Christ. My new self was raised and seated with Him above the forces of evil, and will be united with Him forever.
How can the understanding of this teaching change our lives?
b) What is our part, in view of what Jesus has already done?

**DAY 6** *Ephesians 1:3, 4, 7, 9, 13.*
The words 'in Christ' or 'in him' occur in all these verses. What benefits are described for those who are thus united with Christ?

# QUESTIONS (contd.)

**DAY 7** *Romans 8:35-39.*

Though we have been redeemed by Christ, we may at times be troubled by a feeling of distance from Him, rejection, self-pity or depression. What is the remedy for this?

# NOTES

Christ has redeemed us, not only to have fellowship with Him in heaven eventually, but that we may enjoy fellowship with Him now, and He with us. We shall look at three Bible pictures that make our union with Him clear to us.

## I. THE VINE AND ITS BRANCHES – John 15

Jesus describes our union with Him in this beautiful picture. He, Himself, is the vine. We, who are His, are branches in the vine. Our Father is the one who cares for the vine. I, together with every other believer, am continually partaking of the life of the vine. Perhaps we could consider the sap that brings the life as the Holy Spirit. Jesus speaks of our abiding in Him and He in us. It is I, the branch, that bears the fruit, but only as I remain united to the vine and keep partaking of its life.

Can you begin to grasp the possibilities of a union like this? And the purpose of this union? That we may bear the fruit of the Spirit described in Galatians 5:22-23. And, as we look at that vine, we see that every other Christian is also a branch, and I am joined to my brother and sister as I am joined to Christ. I am also receiving the life of Christ through my brother, and likewise being a vehicle of the outflowing of His life to others.

## 2. THE BODY OF CHRIST – Ephesians 1:22-23; 4:15-16

The church of Jesus is described as a body of which He is the Head. Every part of a healthy body works in co-ordination with every other part, as directed by the head. Each part is reliant on the head for direction. But Jesus, the Head, also needs a body as the vehicle through which to reveal Himself to the world. This is a clear picture of my union with Christ, receiving direction from Him, nourishment through the bloodstream (which could well represent the Holy Spirit), and working in harmonious relationship with every other member of the body.

## 3. MARRIAGE – Revelation 19:7-8

This is the most intimate and a very beautiful picture of our relationship with our Lord. Paul tells us in Romans 7:4 that we have died to the law, our old spouse, that we might be joined (married) to another, to Jesus who was raised from the dead, that together we may bear fruit for God. The marriage relationship, above any, speaks of a partnership of love, caring and sharing.

In the Old Testament in the book of Ruth there is a picture of this very relationship. Boaz, who represents Jesus, became 'goel' or Kinsman-Redeemer to Ruth, a penniless, foreign believer. He redeemed her from poverty, insecurity and obscurity, to become his bride. And together they bore fruit. Yes, Jesus Christ was descended from the unity of these two.

## 4. THE GREAT EXCHANGE

Jesus is our Kinsman-Redeemer. Our Kinsman because He became one of us; our Redeemer because He rescued us from Satan's dominion, that He might claim us as His bride. If we can really believe that His love to us always remains warm and constant, however we may feel, we will begin to learn the secret of abiding in that love, that in union together we may bear fruit for God.

*MEMORY VERSE*:
Remain in me, and I will remain in you. No branch can bear fruit by itself; it must remain in the vine. Neither can you bear fruit unless you remain in me (John 15:4).

# STUDY 9

PRESENT-TENSE SALVATION

## QUESTIONS

**DAY 1** *Titus 3:5; 1 Corinthians 1:18; 1 Peter 1:5.*
a) Can you pick out in these three verses the three tenses of salvation?
b) Comment on these three aspects of salvation.

**DAY 2** *Romans 8:29; 2 Corinthians 3:18; Ephesians 1:12.*
a) What purpose of redemption do these verses emphasise?
b) How does this come about?

**DAY 3** *Ephesians 4:15; 2 Peter 3:18; 2 Thessalonians 1:3.*
a) What idea is present in all these scriptures?
b) What are some of the means God uses to bring us into Christian maturity?
(You might form an analogy by considering how a baby grows to maturity.)

**DAY 4** *Matthew 7:11; John 1:12; Romans 8:15-17; Hebrews 2:7-11; 1 John 3:1-3.*
Because Christ has redeemed you, you have become a child of God. How does the knowledge that God is our Father help us in our Christian walk?

**DAY 5** *Mark 16:15-18; Luke 10:17-19; Acts 3:5, 16; 2 Corinthians 2:14; Colossians 2:9, 10, 15.*
a) How is Satan affected by our redemption?
b) From where does our power to live in victory come?
c) Why then do we not always live victoriously?

**DAY 6** *Matthew 16:24; 1 Corinthians 1:18; Galatians 2:20; 6:14.*
a) We came into salvation through the cross of Christ. What part does the cross play in our ongoing experience of salvation?
b) Paul boasted in the cross of Christ. Do you continually praise God for all that Jesus has accomplished for you on the cross?

# QUESTIONS (contd.)

**DAY 7** *2 Corinthians 5:18-20; Matthew 4:18-20; 28:18-20; Acts 1:8.*
a) God has reconciled us to Himself through Christ. Now, with what special work does He entrust us? Is this a work for a few specially chosen Christians or for all?
b) On whose behalf do I do it?
c) What special enduement of power do I need to do this work effectively?

Many Christians regard salvation as a past- and future-tense experience: 'I have put my trust in Jesus and been forgiven, so I know I have a place reserved in heaven.' Wonderful! But salvation is so much more. Otherwise, the Lord might as well transfer us to heaven the moment we believe! No, we have been left here to experience the fruits of salvation in our day-to-day living, and to be a light to those still in darkness.

Paul speaks of salvation in three tenses:

> You have been saved – Ephesians 2:8
> We are being saved – 2 Corinthians 2:15
> We shall be saved – Romans 5:9

We were saved from sin and condemnation the moment we believed, but we spend a lifetime entering into all that salvation has provided for us. Finally, we reach the climax of salvation when we meet our Lord Jesus and dwell with Him forever.

Paul tells us to work OUT our salvation, for it is God who is working IN us to will and to do His good purpose (Phil. 2:12-13). Let's look at how we can go about working out His salvation in our daily lives.

### 1. BY GROWING IN FAITH
God plants that seed of faith in our hearts when we come to Him. Now that seed must grow. As we meditate on God's Word, its wonderful promises and commands, our faith in Jesus and His presence and power within us will continue to grow. Keep praising God and speaking out His Word, as a stimulant to faith.

### 2. BY GROWING IN HOLINESS
It has been said that we are as holy as we want to be. Provision has been made in the cross of Jesus for us to be redeemed from all sin and become holy people. But so often we choose to go our own way. In order to grow in holiness we must earnestly DESIRE to become like Jesus, and trust the Holy Spirit within us to bring this about. This involves quick repentance when we slip, and faith that the blood of Jesus keeps cleansing us. The old life needs to be continually starved, and the new life fed by fellowship and all that builds us up. Let's believe that a life of obedience to Christ is a life of true fulfilment.

### 3. BY GROWING IN LOVE
Like every other area of our Christian lives, this is a co-operation between God and ourselves. 'God has poured out his love into our hearts by the Holy Spirit, whom he has given us' (Rom. 5:5). Our part is to keep our hearts receptive to

God's love, and to refuse negative and judgmental thoughts of others. Let's face it, we don't always like people, but as we act in love towards them, God's love within us overcomes our negative feelings.

Paul reminded the Thessalonian Christians that they had been taught by God to love one another, 'And in fact, you do love all the brothers ... Yet we urge you ... to do so more and more' (I Thess. 4:10). Jesus told us that God's main requirement is that we love God and others. Grasping the fact that God loves unworthy me is the greatest stimulant to my loving Him, His vast family and those who are His potential children. Love will win them where argument fails. Let's aim to grow in love.

### *MEMORY VERSE*:
Jesus Christ, who gave himself for us to redeem us from all wickedness and to purify for himself a people that are his very own, eager to do what is good (Titus 2:14).

# STUDY 10
## FUTURE-TENSE SALVATION

## QUESTIONS

**DAY 1** *Romans 8:18-23.*
a) What was it that enabled Paul to face the many sufferings he was enduring? (For a list see 2 Cor. 11:23-28.)
b) What is all creation waiting for?
c) I John 3:2 tells us we are now the sons of God. What then is the meaning of Romans 8:19?

**DAY 2** *2 Corinthians 4:16-18.*
a) Though our bodies are weakening, what can increase in strength?
b) Why should eternal values be more important to us than material ones? Are they, in your life?

**DAY 3** *I Corinthians 15:12-26.*
a) Why does Paul so stress the fact of the bodily resurrection of Jesus?
b) What is the contrast between what we inherit from Adam and what we inherit through Christ?

**DAY 4** *I Corinthians 15:42-44, 49; I John 3:2-3.*
a) How are we encouraged to believe that we shall recognise each other in the resurrection (Matt. 17:3-4; John 20:20)?
b) Paul made four comparisons between the body 'sown' and the body 'raised'. What are they?
c) What is the most glorious change that will take place in us when we meet Jesus?

**DAY 5** *John 5:24; I John 5:13.*
If we have been redeemed by Jesus, why do we not need to entertain any doubts about spending eternity with Him?

**DAY 6** *Isaiah 11:11-12; Ezekiel 36:24; Matthew 24:4-14, 29-31.*
a) Although we do not know the day or hour of Christ's return, He has indicated some signs that will precede it (which we cannot go into at length). What are some signs that are being fulfilled today?
b) Comment on the thought that Christians are the only people who can be truly optimistic in this day and age.

# QUESTIONS (contd.)

**DAY 7** *Revelation 21:1-7, 22-27; 22:1-5.*

a) What are some of the most exciting aspects that John records about heaven?

b) Jesus assures us that He will certainly return and invites us to come to Him.

Have you come to Him? Are you ready to greet Him on His return?

The life we are now living is, for all who are in Christ Jesus, a preparation for the glorious life ahead. Paul said, 'If anyone is in Christ, he is a new creation.' When Jesus rose from the dead, He inaugurated an entirely new race of people on the earth. He was the firstborn of that new race through His resurrection from the dead (Rom. 8:29; Col. 1:18; Heb. 12:23), and we become members of that new race through the new birth. Eternal life doesn't start for us after we die, or on Christ's return – we already have it!

John tells us: 'Now we are children of God, and what we will be has not yet been made known. But we know that when he appears, we shall be like him, for we shall see him as he is' (1 John 3:2). At that moment redemption will be completed.

In looking forward to the glorious things that lie ahead, let us be assured that they have already commenced, and let us see ourselves even now in the dignity of sons and daughters of God, members of the new creation, being prepared for eternity with God.

But, although we are enjoying our present-tense salvation, the best is yet to come! Whether we are alive when Jesus returns, or whether we shall have passed on, makes little difference. Suddenly, there will be the triumphant shout of the Lord, the trumpet blast of the archangel, and the Lord will appear in all His glory as He returns to earth to reign (1 Thess. 4:16-18). Then, wonder of wonders, the force of gravity will be reversed, as God's people begin to rise from their graves, and those still alive join them to meet the Lord in the air. No more arthritis or poor eyesight or decaying teeth. Our bodies will be transformed to be like the body our Lord had after His resurrection. Perfect! A body not bound by any of the laws of nature; a body that can never know pain, weakness or death.

There are many interpretations of what precedes and follows that glorious event. Praise God, we don't have to work it all out or understand it perfectly in order to be part of it. Suffice it to say with Paul, 'And so we will be with the Lord forever'. And also with the loved ones who have preceded us. What glorious reunions there will be in His presence.

How will we spend eternity? We don't know. But ... 'No eye has seen, no ear has heard, no mind has conceived what God has prepared for those who love him' (1 Cor. 2:9). Certainly there will be no more boredom in heaven. We shall know complete fulfilment. Eternity will almost be too short to praise our God and Father for such a 'great salvation'. Let's start practising now!

*MEMORY VERSE:*
1 John 3:2 (Quoted above).

# ANSWER GUIDE

The following pages contain an Answer Guide. It is recommended that answers to the questions be attempted before turning to this guide. It is only a guide and the answers given should not be treated as exhaustive.

# GUIDE TO STUDY 1

**DAY 1**   a) 1. God formed Adam's body from the dust of the ground and breathed His own Spirit into him.
2. He formed Eve from the man's body, thus bringing the two into a close relationship.
b) *Perfect spiritually.* He had communion and communication with God.
*Perfect mentally.* He was able to name and subdue the animals, tend the garden, etc.
*Perfect physically.* No evidence of physical imperfection.

**DAY 2**   a) Not to eat from the tree of the knowledge of good and evil. They were to trust God to reveal His will to them.
b) Death.

**DAY 3**   a) He questioned if she had heard correctly: 'Did God really say?' He openly contradicted what God had said: 'You will not surely die.'
b) He implied that God was keeping something from them: 'God knows that when you eat of it ... you will be like God.'

**DAY 4**   a) In her body: good for food; in her mind: a delight to the eyes; in her spirit: would make her wise as God. (Also called by John 'the cravings of sinful man, the lust of his eyes and the boasting of what he has and does'.)
b) Sin (or rebellion).

**DAY 5**   a) They were afraid of Him and hid from Him.
b) Adam blamed his wife Eve (and also God for giving her to him!).
c) Cain became a murderer (our sin always affects others).
d) Eve would have pain in childbirth; Adam would have to do painful manual labour. Both were put out of the garden.

**DAY 6**   a) Sin entered the world bringing death to all. All are born as sinners.
b) They died spiritually that day in that their fellowship with God was severed. Physical decay commenced, eventually leading to physical death.
We have inherited their tendency to sin, with all its consequences of condemnation and death.

**DAY 7**   God promised that the offspring (Jesus) of the woman would crush the serpent's head – Christ defeated Satan through the cross.
God Himself sacrificed an animal in order to clothe Adam and Eve, a further picture of Jesus' sacrifice.

# GUIDE TO STUDY 2

**DAY 1**   a) His son Isaac.
b) God was prepared to offer up Jesus, His beloved and only Son.

**DAY 2**   a) Jesus carried His wooden cross to the place of death.
b) God the Father and Christ the Son together carried out the work of salvation ('God was reconciling the world to himself in Christ' 2 Cor. 5:19).
c) Yes. He could have escaped if he had chosen.

**DAY 3**   a) Isaac did not actually have to die; a substitute was provided. But Jesus actually died on the cross.
b) Abraham told his servants (perhaps not completely understanding what he said) that he and Isaac would worship and return. Isaac symbolically died as he was bound on the altar and his being released from the place of death was like a resurrection.

**DAY 4**   a) The chosen lamb had to be male, young and without any defect or blemish. Jesus fulfilled these requirements: He was sinless.
b) The blood had to be shed and applied to the house. Jesus' blood had to be shed on the cross.

**DAY 5**   a) Shedding the blood was not sufficient – it had to be applied. Although Jesus' blood has been shed, it has no effect until we apply it to our hearts by personally trusting Him.
b) As they partook of the flesh it literally became part of them. So, as we accept Jesus into our lives, He becomes the strength of our lives.

**DAY 6**   a) The celebration of the Holy Communion or the Lord's Supper (or Eucharist), which Jesus Himself inaugurated at the very time of the Jewish Passover.
b) That it is insincere to celebrate the sacrifice of Jesus, which saves us from sin, while deliberately continuing to sin. Jesus is the Bread of Life, who is sinless, and He comes to live within us.

**DAY 7**   a) When we leave Satan's kingdom, Jesus gives us all the spiritual riches of His grace: His presence, enabling, love, comfort, etc.
b) From slavery.
Through Christ's sacrifice, God has redeemed us from slavery to Satan.

# GUIDE TO STUDY 3

**DAY 1**  a) That He would be rejected by the nation and delivered to the Gentiles (Romans) to be mocked, scourged and crucified, but He would be raised to life on the third day. He was giving His life as a ransom for many.

b) It was more than a martyr's death, because He knew He had come into the world for the express purpose of giving His life as a sacrifice for sin, and He had the assurance He would be raised to life again.

**DAY 2**  a) He was innocent.

b) He claimed that He always did what pleased God.

**DAY 3**  a) His appearance was marred beyond human likeness; He was despised and rejected by men.

b) He was stricken, smitten and afflicted by God, as He carried our punishment.

**DAY 4**  a) He bore our sins and sicknesses that we might receive peace and health.

b) He bore His sufferings patiently, and did not attempt to defend Himself.

**DAY 5**  a) He died between two robbers, and a rich man (Joseph) provided a grave for Him.

b) The soldiers pronounced Him dead and pierced His side with a spear to be doubly sure. Joseph and Nicodemus had no doubt, otherwise they would not have wrapped Him in a shroud and left Him in a tomb.

**DAY 6**  a) Verse 10 speaks of prolonging His days – alive for evermore!
Verse 11 speaks of seeing the result of His sufferings (a great company of believers) and being satisfied.
Verse 12 speaks of being given a place of greatness.

b) Jesus gained a great company of believers, His Church.
We who believe are justified, acquitted and counted righteous in God's sight.

**DAY 7**  a) Jesus appeared to:
Mary Magdalene; a group of women; ten apostles (Thomas absent and Judas dead); Peter; two on their way to Emmaus; eleven apostles,

together with the two from Emmaus; the disciples while fishing on the Lake of Galilee; to James; to five hundred at once; to the group at the Ascension; and later to Paul.

b) If He arose from the dead, then He is alive and active today. His resurrection proves that God accepted His sacrifice, Satan has been defeated and we are free. His resurrection is the guarantee that we too shall be resurrected, with an immortal, perfect body like His.

# GUIDE TO STUDY 4

**DAY 1**  a) Repentance – the need to be sorry for and turn away from sin.
b) We are to show by our changed lives that we have truly repented.

**DAY 2**  a) To feel sorry for having done something wrong. (Similar definitions in different dictionaries.)
Yes, it is more than a feeling of sorrow, it includes a change of attitude.
b) No.
c) Being unwilling to forgive others.

**DAY 3**  a) He left the old life, returned to the father and confessed his sin honestly.
b) He was forgiven and received as a son by a loving father.

**DAY 4**  a) Believing or putting our faith in Jesus as Saviour and Lord.
b) 'Saving faith' is trust in Jesus and surrender to Him, resulting in a changed life. 'Head belief' is merely mental assent and produces no change in the life.

**DAY 5**  a) Receiving Jesus.
b) He will come into the life of the one who receives Him.

**DAY 6**  a) Acknowledging Him before outsiders; also acknowledging Him to the church (e.g. confirmation, adult baptism, etc.).
b) That He has become my Saviour and Lord.

**DAY 7**  a) Because God Himself has promised it and He cannot lie.
b) Yes, but to varying degrees in different people. Some people experience very little in the way of feelings apart from the assurance that God has accepted them; others experience great feelings of joy.
No. The Word and promises of God are what we must rely on. Feelings are not constant, and can change continually.
c) Personal.

# GUIDE TO STUDY 5

**DAY 1**
a) Convict of sin (guilt).
b) 'Granted' and 'gift' show that they come from God.

**DAY 2**
a) We are born again, we experience the new birth.
b) The Holy Spirit.
c) The Holy Spirit comes upon us with His own life, causing us to be born again as sons (and daughters) of God.

**DAY 3**
a) He writes our names in the Lamb's Book of Life in heaven.
b) The Spirit of God within us causes us to know God as Father.

**DAY 4**
a) The Holy Spirit, who is also referred to as the Spirit of God and of Christ (Rom. 8:9).
b) It should make us realise that we have all the power within us to enable us to live the Christian life. We don't have to struggle to live it in our own strength.

**DAY 5**
He would be our teacher, would guide us into all truth, would cause us to understand events still to come, and would glorify Jesus in and through our lives.

**DAY 6**
Love, joy, peace, patience, kindness, goodness, faithfulness, gentleness, self-control.

**DAY 7**
a) The Bible states clearly that God has provided only one means of coming to God, and that is Jesus Christ.
b) In every other religion, people have to try to earn salvation by their good works, and never have any assurance that they have obtained it. Jesus gives it as a free gift to be received. It is by grace, not by merit.

# GUIDE TO STUDY 6

**DAY 1**
a) Slavery to sin, guilt, hopelessness, self-centredness, bad habits, fears, etc.

b) Sin separated us from God, but through Christ we have been reconciled with God. Christ took the separation away when He took our sin upon Himself on the cross.

**DAY 2**
a) In forgiveness the penalty for sin is set aside; in justification God treats us as righteous for the sake of Christ.

b) On the cross Jesus took not only the punishment, but the guilt of our sins. The righteousness of Christ is put to our account.

c) This can lead to differing viewpoints. For some these verses mean that Jesus suffered physically as well as spiritually for us and therefore provision is made for physical as well as spiritual well-being. Many factors keep us back from entering fully into this provision. Others would limit these verses to a more spiritual application.

**DAY 3**
a) Life instead of death.
Reigning in life instead of slavery to sin and death.

b) Receiving as a gift God's grace and righteousness.

**DAY 4**
a) No.

b) Because we believe that Jesus has already suffered our punishment.

**DAY 5**
Blessing in place of a curse.
Christ's riches in place of poverty.

**DAY 6**
Everlasting life; abundant life.
Victorious life (reigning in life).
Christ is our life.

**DAY 7**
a)

| | |
|---|---|
| Our death | His life |
| Our sin | His righteousness |
| Our sickness | His health |
| Our poverty | His riches |
| Our old nature | His new nature |

b) Personal.

# GUIDE TO STUDY 7

**DAY 1**     a) To preach good news to the poor, proclaim freedom for the prisoners, recovery of sight for the blind, to release the oppressed.
b) From the power of Satan to God; from the dominion of darkness into the Kingdom of God's Son.
c) When Jesus paid the price for us on the cross, but it becomes ours when we receive Christ's salvation.

**DAY 2**     a) From slavery to sin.
b) Recognise that it has come about through Christ's death. Refuse to yield to Satan's enticements. Yield ourselves to God, as our new Master.

**DAY 3**     a) Death.
b) Eternal life.

**DAY 4**     a) They were returning again to a life of bondage by trying to keep the law.
b) Having faith in Jesus, and receiving His righteousness.
c) To stand firm in Christ's freedom and refuse to submit to bondage to Satan.

**DAY 5**     a) By the Holy Spirit.
b) Rigid bondage to forms and ceremonies in church worship; considering certain types of clothing necessary for attending meetings; considering Sunday the equivalent to the Jewish Sabbath with its rigid restrictions, etc. Rigidity and inflexibility in externals, resulting in lack of love and in judging of others.

**DAY 6**     a) Fear should be replaced by love, power and self-control. These are available as we look to Christ when fear assails us.
b) God becomes our Father.

**DAY 7**     One of recognising and acknowledging Christ as our Lord, and bringing Him love, worship and obedience.

# GUIDE TO STUDY 8

**DAY 1**    Through Christ's death, He has brought us into a new covenant relationship. On Christ's part there is love, faithfulness, protection, provision, leadership. On our part, love, faithfulness, trust, obedience. It is a permanent relationship and results in fruitfulness.

**DAY 2**    a) The picture of two oxen working together under the yoke.
b) It needs training.
c) To restfulness.

**DAY 3**    a) On abiding or remaining in Christ (v. 5).
b) Our prayers are answered (v. 7).
c) By keeping Christ's commands (vv. 10, 11).

**DAY 4**    a) With fellow Christians and with the Father, the Son and the Spirit.
b) We can talk to God in prayer, and He talks to us by His Spirit and through the Word.

**DAY 5**    a) It causes us to know that, as Christ was triumphant over evil, so I, too, have that power since I am united with Him.
b) To refuse the old temptations as they arise, and to receive the fact of the victorious life of Christ within me.

**DAY 6**    We have every spiritual blessing. We have holiness, forgiveness, wisdom, the knowledge of His will and we have the indwelling Holy Spirit as a promise of our full inheritance in heaven.

**DAY 7**    Our faith must be in the assurance of God's Word, not in our feelings. We must refuse those negative feelings and praise God for the assurance He gives of His constant love. (This usually dispels the darkness.)

# GUIDE TO STUDY 9

**DAY 1**  a) Titus 3:5  – past tense.
I Corinthians 1:18 – present tense.
I Peter 1:5  – future tense.
b) We were saved when we received Jesus. The process of being saved (or being sanctified) continues through life. Our salvation (or glorification) will be completed when we see Jesus and become like Him.

**DAY 2**  a) To become like Jesus.
b) After we receive Jesus and as we keep looking to Him by faith, the indwelling Holy Spirit brings about this change in our lives.

**DAY 3**  a) Growth.
b)
| | |
|---|---|
| Feeding | – Reading and digesting God's Word. |
| Crying | – Longing to know God better as we pray to Him. |
| Learning to walk | – To walk in the Spirit in obedience. |
| Learning to talk | – Witnessing about Jesus. |
| Exercise | – Practical Christian work. |
| Mixed feeding | – Deeper understanding of the Lord. |
| Playing | – Christian fellowship including social activities. |

**DAY 4**  Because God is our Father we know that He loves us and so we can trust His dealings in our lives. He delights to answer our prayers. This knowledge of God as Father gives us a sense of worth, and a sense of the worth of all His other children. It brings about the family spirit within the church.

**DAY 5**  a) We no longer belong to him; he has no authority over us; we can see others delivered from his power.
b) From Christ who defeated Satan.
c) Because we forget to look to Christ for victory, or deliberately choose to go our own way. The Lord will never override our free will.

**DAY 6**  a) We recognise in the cross that our old life has been put to death, and we walk in the power of Christ's resurrection life. The cross also includes being prepared to suffer for Christ's sake – He did not promise us an easy life.

b) Personal.

**DAY 7**    a) The work of reconciling others to God through Christ.
For all.
b) On Christ's behalf since we are His representatives on earth.
c) The power of the Holy Spirit.

# GUIDE TO STUDY 10

**DAY 1**
a) Anticipation of the glory that was to come.
b) The final stage of redemption, when we receive our new bodies.
c) We will be declared as God's sons (and daughters) before all creation. (The Greek word here translated sons, 'huios', means adult sons – we shall have reached spiritual maturity.)

**DAY 2**
a) Our inner man or our spirits.
b) Material values are temporary, they can't be taken with us. As the word implies, eternal values will last forever.
Personal.

**DAY 3**
a) Because Christ's resurrection is a guarantee of our resurrection.
b) Through Adam we inherit death; through Christ, life.

**DAY 4**
a) The disciples recognised Jesus (except where it was stated that their eyes were kept from recognising Him – Luke 24:16). He still had the marks of the nails visible in His body. Also Moses and Elijah were recognisable.
b) Sown perishable, in dishonour, in weakness, a mere physical body.
Raised imperishable, in glory, in power, a spiritual body.
c) We shall be perfect like Him.

**DAY 5**
Jesus declared that if we believe in Him we shall not be condemned. We are already in His Kingdom, and can know it by His promise and by His Spirit within us.

**DAY 6**
a) The return of the Jews to their land.
Wars, famines, earthquakes, persecutions, rise of false cults. Increase in wickedness, yet an increase in the spread of the gospel worldwide. Signs in the heavens (space travel?), etc.
b) Only Christians have the assurance that the next life is better than this.
Only Christians know that Christ will return to earth and that He alone has the answer to problems that world rulers cannot handle.

**DAY 7**
a) God will dwell with His people. No more mourning, sorrow, pain; drinking continually of the water of life (complete satisfaction and fulfilment); knowing God intimately as Father; eating of the fruit of the tree of life (contrast Genesis 3:24); nothing evil; pure

worship of and service to God; constantly seeing God, and having His Name stamped upon us; no night; reigning with God over the universe forever!
b) Personal.

# NOTES

# NOTES

# NOTES

# THE WORD WORLDWIDE

We first heard of WORD WORLDWIDE over 20 years ago when Marie Dinnen, its founder, shared excitedly about the wonderful way ministry to one needy woman had exploded to touch many lives. It was great to see the Word of God being made central in the lives of thousands of men and women, then to witness the life-changing results of them applying the Word to their circumstances. Over the years the vision for WORD WORLDWIDE has not dimmed in the hearts of those who are involved in this ministry. God is still at work through His Word and in today's self-seeking society, the Word is even more relevant to those who desire true meaning and purpose in life. WORD WORLDWIDE is a ministry of WEC International, an interdenominational missionary society, whose sole purpose is to see Christ known, loved and worshipped by all, particularly those who have yet to hear of His wonderful name. This ministry is a vital part of our work and we warmly recommend the WORD WORLDWIDE 'Geared for Growth' Bible studies to you. We know that as you study His Word you will be enriched in your personal walk with Christ. It is our hope that as you are blessed through these studies, you will find opportunities to help others discover a personal relationship with Jesus. As a mission we would encourage you to work with us to make Christ known to the ends of the earth.

Stewart and Jean Moulds – British Directors, **WEC International.**

A full list of over 50 'Geared for Growth' studies can be obtained from:

**ENGLAND**  John and Ann Edwards
5 Louvain Terrace, Hetton-le-Hole, Tyne & Wear, DH5 9PP
Tel. 0191 5262803 Email: rhysjohn.edwards@virgin.net

**IRELAND**  Steffney Preston
33 Harcourts Hill, Portadown, Craigavon, N. Ireland, BT62 3RE
Tel. 028 3833 7844 Email: sa.preston@talk21.com

**SCOTLAND** Margaret Halliday
10 Douglas Drive, Newton Mearns, Glasgow, G77 6HR
Tel. 0141 639 8695 Email: m.halliday@ntlworld.com

**WALES**  William and Eirian Edwards
Penlan Uchaf, Carmarthen Road, Kidwelly, Carms., SA17 5AF
Tel. 01554 890423 Email: Penlan.uchaf@farming.co.uk

## UK CO-ORDINATOR

Anne Jenkins
2 Windermere Road, Carnforth, Lancs., LA5 9AR
Tel. 01524 734797 Email: anne@jenkins.abelgratis.com

**UK Website: www.wordworldwide.org.uk**

# Christian Focus Publications

publishes books for all ages

Our mission statement –
STAYING FAITHFUL
In dependence upon God we seek to help make His infallible word, the Bible, relevant. Our aim is to ensure that the Lord Jesus Christ is presented as the only hope to obtain forgiveness of sin, live a useful life and look forward to heaven with Him.
REACHING OUT
Christ's last command requires us to reach out to our world with His gospel. We seek to help fulfill that by publishing books that point people towards Jesus and help them to develop a Christ-like maturity. We aim to equip all levels of readers for life, work, ministry and mission.

Books in our adult range are published in three imprints.
*Christian Focus* contains popular works including biographies, commentaries, basic doctrine, and Christian living. Our children's books are also published in this imprint.
*Mentor* focuses on books written at a level suitable for Bible College and seminary students, pastors, and other serious readers; the imprint includes commentaries, doctrinal studies, examination of current issues, and church history.
*Christian Heritage* contains classic writings from the past.

For details of our titles visit us on our website
www.christianfocus.com

ISBN 0 908067 20 8

Copyright © WEC International

Published in 2002 by
Christian Focus Publications, Geanies House,
Fearn, Ross-shire, IV20 ITW, Scotland
and
WEC International, Bulstrode, Oxford Road,
Gerrards Cross, Bucks , SL9 8SZ

Cover design by Alister MacInnes

Printed and bound by J.W Arrowsmith, Bristol